Atoms,
Soul Music
and other poems

Baron Wormser

Thanks to the National Endowment for the Arts

Acknowledgments
Some of these poems originally appeared in *The Black Fly Review,*
Embers, Harper's, The Manhattan Review, Michigan Quarterly Review, The
Paris Review, New England Review and Bread Loaf Quarterly, Poetry,
Washington Review, The Yale Review

Published by British American Publishing
3 Cornell Road
Latham, NY 12110
Manufactured in the United States of America

94 93 92 91 90 5 4 3 2 1

Library of Congress Cataloging in Publication Data

Wormser, Baron.
    Atoms, soul music and other poems / Baron Wormser.
        p. cm.
    ISBN 0-945167-14-8 : $7.95
    I. Title.
PS3573.0693A96   1989
811'.54—dc19

88-34545
CIP

For Janet, Maisie, Owen, and Sherry

Contents

II

I

The Questions of Children

Answering the questions of children is as easy
As a moment, as dim as deliberation,
As reductive as hope. Ducks can both swim and fly,
Autos run on gasoline, the moon
Is much farther away than it seems.

So it goes with the available *known,*
That candidate who's always there,
Oblivious to the greater meanings, fawning
On facts while tones and pauses signal truth or lie.

The child makes do, understanding that
Answers are good for more than answers
As ducks are better than words.

Like weather, wonder returns.
The child crawls in you for a bed,

Listens for a place where mystery is learned.

Nightmare

Even our habitual sanity,
The reconciling flesh, falters.
We nuzzle and rub and embrace
The screaming child but the nerves

Are elsewhere and when the terror
Subsides it is time, not love,
That has been the nurse.
Dutifully we continue to stroke

And soothe, say a few lopsided words,
Knowingly unavailing, tuck in the
Dreadful. Then sleep again.
We lie awake, afraid

Of this inconclusiveness. Our
Firm place is nowhere and
The assurances of light seem glib
And duplicitous, lures of appearance

Which we too gladly sip. Now,
As the body tires, edges
And depths break like the ice
Of an arctic pack and no gesture

Redeems the menace of our comfort:
Faith is dark, we must give in.

Married Sex

The jokes about aspirins and the late-night news
Ring a little less-than-true.
The body avoids itself and what it once knew.
Any economist will tell you:
Wage slaves don't make love, they screw.

Some modern help is always forthcoming—
Yet fantasy finds repetition a dry thing,
While technique is too much like acting.
Familiar flesh mumbles more than sings,
Orgasm is an accountable blessing.

How easily the accustomed becomes a dream
As sheets and sweat and groans create a scene
That is apt and strange, that stagnates and careens.
Time isn't as tight as it seems:
The arching moment robs what it redeems,

And two people are left with their shares
Of fractional bliss. The phallus says it cares,
The vagina agrees. Don't try to repair
This masque of passion. Coitus tires of dares.
When need is cordial, desire is prepared.

The Single Urge

Peggy Everett, my first girl friend, explains
That she is not so much leaving me as going
To someone else. I look at her as if
She were a mountain peak in the next county.
Later I try to educate the mirror in my room
But the mirror is not interested. It is only me
On a certain day, short in stature and short
Of knowledge, keen on the brazen inconsequence of desire.

I stay up late and try to imagine what it
Is like to be in her body. How can pleasure be
Confused? We had agreed, and I still agree
With the single urge that looks out windows, writes
Names in the margins of notebooks and is always
Ready to merge with what it lacks, what it believes.

Kitchen, 1952

1

It was the kitchen of that
New house to which she moved
In 1952
That proved to my mother
The strength of her ascent.

The world was hers in a room
Possessed of an oracular
Cleanliness, all surfaces ready
To stand the test of any
Amount of dissolute life,
All doors and drawers and appliances
Instantly capable.

The plastic clock in the shape
Of an apple might have smiled
Without educated irony
Upon this smiling housewife.
Modernity was a domestic dream.

2

Each generation tells a tale
Of well-being which
The next generation intently
Eviscerates. Each era
Sanctifies its invention
Of human health.

To my mother, the full-
Color pictures must
Have spoken plainly,
Momentarily timeless,
Poised on the peak of a fond
But affordable hope.

She looked about her,
Unbewildered, serene with
The wisdom of her female calling.
The silent kitchen answered.

3

We children shrieked at spinach,
Sawed our way through roasts,
Clamored for the sugary
Vapors of packaged cake mix.
Dad came home late from work again.

Our little deaths are so
Predictable, yet they remain
Strange to us. The counters
And pots were cleared and cleaned
In the wheel of ancient work.
Daily, love shone and disappeared.

Another family heals
And fractures now in that
Solicitous kitchen.
My mother's life stands out
With all the overwrought truth
Of disappointment, the promise
That so gradually broke.

Deviled eggs and fried
Chicken and fruit punch
Sit on the table

One languid June day.
My mother laughs as if
To mock her own perfection,
As if to say, "But look at
Our hunger, it is incomplete."

Social Security

Each month a check, and my grandmother's born-
Again turmoil, tears ranging from
   Foreshortened sobs of relief,
   Her old age enthroned
On the far shores of comfort—a suburban
Home full of cookies, sliced bread, and tv's—
To tense, declamatory grief that ended in
   Tranquilizers and two
   Incommunicado days in bed.
All things had been possible in America.
Now there was this rectangular mélange—a little
Money, an official number, and some punched-out
Squares that only made sense to machines.

Chances were I'd have to listen to the story
Of Shana Rosenblatt who led a strike
Of seamstresses in 1913 and had her
Arms broken by company thugs. Shana
   Was dead, but the government
   Wanted Grandma to live.
It did not cheer her up. For a dollar I
   Was willing to hear her
   Talk about Eugene Debs.
Even at the age of ten I understood
That America could only choose between
What is and what is—none of this
What-might-be stuff. What was it like

To break the arms of a shrieking woman? The men
Must have needed money badly. Perhaps they had
   Sick children at home.
   America had been full
Of sick children once. Grandma's sister, Reva,

Had died in an epidemic. Now if
We had a cough or sore throat we went
To Doctor Katz. Who could imagine a child dying?
    I turned on the tv,
        And we watched James Garner
Reluctantly shoot a cheating braggard. Grandma cheered
And told me I needed a Stetson hat. She would
Buy me one. Only Americans wore hats like that.

    "This money is people,"
        She'd say when she gave
Me a dollar. I made out that I understood.
After all, there was a man's face on it.
Did George Washington know that he
Was going to become money? It must
Have been a funny feeling if he did.
Once, I took the bill and tore it up
    To see if it would put
        Itself back together,
To see if it had a life of its own. My grand-
Mother told me I was a fool and looked
At the pieces on the carpeted floor and spat.

1967

It was a summer for sitting naked in
The backyard, the deep drizzle deploying the young
As an aspect of the lately discovered elemental.
Too cool and damp for lyrical bouts,
Bodies gained gravity and pondered

The ease of dissolution while dirt, grass,
And the soft spume of slugs stuck to flesh.
The neighbors were appalled, confused, bothered,
And resigned the way people are
In assassination times.

You might as well argue with the night
Though mothers and fathers still stormed,
Invoking Bible and country and the *ne*
Plus ultra of bourgeois security.
How hateful is the finickiness of exaggeration,

The wish to merge with the unavoidable!
Good sense goes out the window for a reason.
Those huge white worms adrift on a solid sea
Gathered dew and immediacy
While the government stayed inside

Honing its grudges, complaining in orders.
It could have been a parable with all
The coveted distance of literature but
The moist joy clung like Eden,
The pained, pierced voices fell down like rain.

Soul Music

The Baltimore evening I saw
Otis and Aretha I knew
Kings and queens existed after all:
Something good and true and danceable,
The uncharted earthbound hit.

They said to believe and leap.
The nation no longer was diagrammatic;
Unsevered feeling fit
Into anybody's skin.
Unthwarted sound was the test
Of embodied, unchurched progress.

Outside that night
Plate glass fractured like
A sobbing final tone,
A plea which brought white men
To the city on a Sunday afternoon
To watch the condemned frolic
At everyone's expense.

Whole blocks burned gladly,
The stuff of democratic
Promise freely redeemed,
The grandeur of performance
Burlesqued by riot.

I, too, protested:
Hadn't I been good,
Hadn't I endorsed
Both sympathy and force?
Didn't I love the music
As much as I could?

On the televised streets
I saw people dancing,
Souls on fire with a passion
That sang of days
No ticket could touch.

1968

The flowers that festooned both hair and tanks
   Would wilt, announced
   The pundits of social horticulture.
The screams arising from truncheons and notions
Of comity would evaporate like a poetical mist.

Sense would return to earth in the form of
   A bargained handshake.
   Consider that if to all things
There is a season, it may be wise to wring
The season's neck. The citizenry, after all,

Already were watching staged apocalypses nightly.
   They could be counted on
   To dismiss these sloganeers
Who didn't have to get up early the next
Morning. Protest is an unemployed luxury.

In the jails, thieves and pimps complained about
   This new element—
   "Utopian scum," as *Pravda*
Forthrightly put it, a phrase too ideological
For American tastes, but one whose heart was in

The properly admonitory place.
   The nations overrun
   By hippies flaunting love,
Not a very attractive sight even

If this absence of bras gave more
Than one deskbound Don Juan a daydream.
   Perhaps, as the pundits
   Reflected, the worst portion

Of foolery is that the fool believes
What he or she is doing. The fool does not know

Any better. Perhaps this is a farce or tragedy.
     Thank God or Lenin
     That the mother and the father
Were there to take such children by their hands,
Advise and cajole, restore civility

To unhappy Prague and Chicago.
     Remember that
     Wardheelers and partyliners
Can make common cause as easily
As the fanciers of guitars and autonomy.

A little fright goes a long way.
     Soon, the pundits
     Proclaimed, there would be
Better smiles: crisp ones like new money,
Avuncular ones like old speeches, savvy ones

Ripe with self-regard. The pundits of social horticulture
     Predicted that pundits
     Would thrive on these more normal
Days, living to give praise to the sturdy stalk
That bears no flowers, drops no seeds in no fresh wind.

1969

Cynical millenarian, I like
You in this shot, posed without
Insignia or emblems,
Just a plain white tee-shirt

And house-painter's pants
Because that is what you are,
An anonymous workman
In the first year of the

Reign of Richard Nixon,
No longer a peace-sign kid
Yet still smoking a j
Each evening for old time's sake,

An accommodation of ecstasy.
The uncertain fun is over,
The wages of definition
Must be paid,

A spontaneous decade ends
In the scrape of the putty
Knife, the money that makes
One week talk to another.

You could be elsewhere
And you know it
But your smile remains.
A false perpetuum sets in

Of Saturday night beers,
Second-hand paperbacks, lengthy
Letters, and pragmatic affairs.
In your hand is your cap

And now it seems that
You too were a soldier,
That this wariness will
Never go away and that

That is a fact, like an
Address, like the neat
Inscription: "Draft dodger
Turns twenty-two today."

In a Cab

Delighted at rush hour
To flaunt his emigré wisdom,
The Russian cabbie tells me that
This country

Is heaven: jazz, enough food,
No whispering,
Cars that work. He smells of onion
And cheap hair cream, wears

A tweed cap. What is the American
Politics of belabored possibility to him?
He is no degreed utopian.
The radio goes from Stan Getz to

A Coltrane hymn; through the steamy windows
The goodness of what is random,
The busy vapors of Sixth Avenue seep in.
Confusion and compromise, brief principle

And bent belief
Are the cloth of this congested life.
The *Post*'s headlines proclaim, but here,
The worst reprobates, both left and right,

Remain men and women, the stuff
Of plain-speaking, self-satisfied sloth.
Taking the long view down this democratic avenue,
My driver gestures with

His middle finger and hits the brakes.
We swear at the buses and Bolsheviks.
Coleman Hawkins sets out. Salt
And honey, that is our state.

Dropping Acid at Aunt Bea and Uncle Harry's 40th Wedding Anniversary Celebration

The little candles which dot the rosette-bedecked
Sheetcake sway so demurely that the happy
Huffing and puffing comes as a cosmic surprise,
An operatic act of gods. What a wind is this breath!
Their eccentric niece, the one who went out West
But flew back for the party, still can see the flames
But tells no one. The flames are Aunt Bea and Uncle Harry.
They stand slightly wavering in the draught of the years
But lambent nonetheless, pleased to have survived
When others just as notable and kind have died.
When they kiss their errant niece, she is burnt but it
Feels good to be branded by these reconciled lives.
Each plastic glass contains a rolling sea.
Each hors d'oeuvres plate is green and greasy.
Bea's sister, Dora, is crying passionately, staring
From her folding seat into an abyss of joy.
Soon it will be time for dancing.
This means a bald accordianist and
A toupéed, still Sinatra-smitten vocalist.
The niece starts tapping her spoon on a coffee cup.
She knows that the room will dance in that earnest
Way that rooms dance. The building will kick in too
And the street won't want to be left out nor will
The automobiles which have been standing around
For hours patiently waiting—they love locomotion.
Bea and Harry take the first steps and it feels
Like the dance of life: feet beating the floor,

Arms entwined, bulging torsos bearing rhythm.
Everyone is suffused with music.
The niece forgets her extremities, her rises and falls.
Everything is actual, for once and for all.

Adultery

One steamy afternoon she steps out of her dress.
Far below, cabs continue to almost collide.
The windowful of scattered enormity
Before him is always palpably personal,
The scrabble of misplaced history.

He turns to see a woman fold a slip.
Lust is helpless intelligence.

Sweetly unnerved, they seem to merge
Into one agreed recognition.
The city evinces its same relentless pain
While they drowse and chat and muse.
They laugh at their mingled courage.

If there is no going backward, there is
No need to strike a moral pose.
Disillusion is easily gratified,
The sighs that are the steps of time
Wilt like the flowers that both have
Forgotten to place in water.

U-Haul

After sharing a bowl of hash, numerous
Poignant and ridiculous anecdotes of
Leave-taking, and the three jokes they knew
About truckers, trucking, or trucks, they began
To settle into the hard plastic seat
And visually explicate the fabulous road—

As in asphalt, a concoction of hydrocarbons
Doled out by huge machines manned by
Superfluous, swaggering men and painted functionally.
As recent liberal arts graduates they
Were unswayed by the claims of utility.
The chief product of life was commentary.

Interstate travel was a rapid disfunction
To be mocked and enjoyed like those
Greasy tubs of chicken and fries.
They burped and swallowed more No-Doz.
There remained nothing sweeter than a coke
Made from syrup and possible lives.
The houses hiding passions and fear
Behind aluminum, vinyl, and stucco

Beckoned like a love note discovered in
A newspaper ad. One night in a cheap motel
They watched tv and balled in the shower.
Lights out, they wondered about drivers
Going by this place and noticing the sign,
The yellow bulbs, the moths in their rare hour.

Embracing a Cloud: Rural Commune, 1971

Who'd known about soybean stew or what
A camshaft did or how asparagus grew?
Even the much-mowed grass was new to those
Who'd wandered once where easy-listening remotely
Shilled the subconscious, floors were buffed daily,
And clerks grimaced their way to coffee breaks.
The precise anonymity of affluence seemed,
If not deadly, then less-than-alive.
A new age was wanted—being an old age most
Were glad to see go by—yet a new age now.
If it had been, as the grandfolks recalled, too cruel,
Yet that had been its beauty too.
If such a life were now not necessity
But something freely fashioned, perhaps
Such freedom could stanch aggrievement and seed
The ultimate back-to-the-land conspiracy.
Off they went—emboldened, generous, and unversed.

Who'd guessed how various this earth is?
Not merely as amusement—the sweet stuff of spring
And all—but as a literal nourishment; tutelage
To slay the irony of self-awareness, once and
For all; incitement to long reflection;
And defiant essence of unlaunderable grime.
You could get lost for days in such environs:
The falling, unfallen barn; the apple trees
Given over to the deer decades ago;
The animals who graciously lived and darkly died.
Even the sky spoke an enumerative tongue,
No longer a backdrop but an active lesson.
Embracing a cloud, they lived among actual signs—
Sun dogs, mares' tails, the last accurate fancies
And the first.

How long does any season last?
Longer than you'd think yet never long enough.
They held hands and bodies, made babies, tried
To subscribe to the current Democrat hopes:
Uncertain Gene McCarthy, the remaining Kennedy,
Plain McGovern. All the tv talk seemed remote:
They had become Americans who worked.
Détente did not augur a new era
For this unmapped sideshow taking place
On a dirt road off another dirt road.
Like nations, each of them moved in
A disparate, self-absorbed motion.
Together, they watched their youth skitter
And pop like a drop on a hot stove.
One grey morning a car, water pump,
Typewriter, chain saw, and adult's leg all broke.
As someone observed at the table that night,
Leaving was inaccurate as staying.

Where is our mending to be accomplished?
In fact, any place your ass calls home,
As in a pair of jeans patched with a pair
That can't be patched anymore—a careful
Custom left over from the heyday of relevance.
Save what you can—though yours will never be mine,
Anything we share makes for a household.

Pigeons

Even naturalists are uninterested in the pigeons
Who loiter everywhere in the cities,
Birds who have sullied themselves
By learning to live with man.
They prosper amid degradation;
They are solicitous and indifferent, unanxious;
They feel they will live another day.
Their instincts are attuned
To the current extent of prodigal carelessness.

Kernels of whimsical saintliness
Fall from the hands of old men and women
Dipping into paper bags full
Of peanuts, bread crusts, fruit peels, seeds.
Like myths, pigeons eat everything.
They are impolite, refuse to be beautiful.
Often they are particolored in invariably unattractive ways.
Old people fondle them with words,
Gurgles, gestures, litanies.
The pigeons congregate like gangs,
Strut like overweight soldiers, shit, and make
An officious mockery of flight.

Their tamed birdiness calls to our humanness.
They offer odd sounds, caricatures, the riches of self-
        absorption.

Listen to their vague digestion,
To their thoughts that are tiny as silica.
Adroit as settlers,

Neither romantics nor classicists,
The pigeons cover corporate plazas, benches, curbs,
    walkways,
Unconcerned with agony,
Grinding corn, investigating the wonders of gum.

Near Skowhegan

In the late October light
The town and mill and river glow
With a good-for-nothing beauty.
All magnitude is here in
The light of emptiness and fullness,
The cup the sun drains everyday.
Stand still and you can feel it:
The wind honing the shore,
The glare crazy on the glass panes,
A pointed chill in the air.
Exhilarating, how no one cares.
Once the water made the mill go,
And people watched the river closely.
Once the town held a promise
Of free-born prosperity.
Now it's a place to work
For those who only know work
In its faultiest sense.
When the shift lets out, everyone
Sniffs at this air, amazingly
Clear and clean and sweet.
Some hold the attitude for seconds,
Then open their car doors carefully
As if entering a vault.

Lament Upon the Closing of the Northern Conservatory in Bangor, Maine

When I pick up the map of a city,
I look first to see if there is a conservatory.
There will always be
Armories, city halls, dumps, ball fields,
But a home for music is not a tax-paying necessity.
I am sad for the city
Which lacks the lesson music preserves:
Form amends our laboring nerves.

Without this blessing, plain life grows eager and soft.
The handshaking brio of feckless energy
Taints all contentment;
Simple gain becomes a reason.
Musicians, we must remember, could have done otherwise.
Instead, they chose this solitude that flowers,
All mere frustration funnelled
Into an hour or two of studied power.
Erring or swift, fingers remain fingers,
Yet the famous frozen music of mortar rises and falls and
fades.
The red bricks are a little graver.
No longer do people intuit what they can't completely do.
No longer are tempers lost and restored.
Hope is not looked for.
I am afraid of how cold it is in the cold winter
Without the genius of the little conservatory!
A busy silence sits on the city.
Places are palpable, but no one has ever
Inhabited one of Schubert's songs.
The chance to visit some small perfection has gone.

Back Road Incident

I'm felling trees, next winter's wood, when I hear
An engine out on the road, a whine that veers
Into a hemorrhaging groan. Wheels spin—
A machine in something it shouldn't be in.
I know the spot, below the bend where the ditch
Is not a ditch and run-off water sits
Throughout the month of March and waits.
I guess a compact with out-of-state plates,
Put the saw down, and begin to walk.
They are out of the car, the sound of anxious talk
Reaches towards me. I emerge from the woods
And wave. The front tires are in good.
I say that I notice that they're stuck.
They begin to narrate the history of their bad luck,
How other things have happened to them in the past—
They have had flat tires, they have run out of gas
When all they wanted to do was admire
The countryside and become inspired.
I get afraid that they're going to cry
And say not to fret, that I will try
To pull them out and go get the '41
Farmall which I bought for two hun-
Dred dollars two rainy springs ago.
It goes, but it goes awfully slow,
And their faces show doubt that it will work—
I may not be an adroit farmer but a jerk
Who is about to pull their bumper off.
The tractor hefts the weight out of that soft
Thick veil of stippled ooze. My friends cheer
And ask me what it's like to live up here.
Muddy in spring. I now have two ruts
In the road which I will spend months
Avoiding. Occasionally I will curse. Maybe

The town will fill them come summer, maybe
They won't. I hear water's suck and seep.
The earth is sobbing. Goodbye, they beep.

The Wormsers Live in a House
Without Electricity

The Wormsers don't know
Kilowatts from their elbows.
    They are radicals, 60s types;
    They are obstructionists.
    They have to go outside to piss.
    They worship the light

That comes up over the pines.
They have lost their purchasing minds.
    At night they sit around the table
    And sketch, write letters, read,
    Complain, tell jokes, pick their teeth,
    Discuss life in terms of a fable.

Is it better or worse?
Is it the stuff of romantic verse,
    Evocations of a world happily lost,
    Or mere role playing, the dialectic
    Of bourgeois rejection, a trick
    They play on themselves at uncertain cost?

At night the howling energy
Of winds, stars, coyotes.
    Always the stubborn labor of eyes
    And hands. It is getting dark
    And the Wormsers sit around a spark
    Set in the middle of a human sky.

Starting the First Fire, Autumn

For Janet

Once again we start to act hospitably.
Today we blacked the stove, swept up
The spiders from the woodbox, split kindling.
Tonight's frost recalls debilities
More thorough than a chill or twinge.
We didn't perish like plants; we weren't house flies:
The pungence of brevity was our false pride.

Now warmth suffices for philosophy,
The fire says that it is the fire it was before,
That there is really just one fire, the way
There is only a single earth or sky.
My hand in the light is faintly freckled, but
Age doesn't figure in this basic mathematic.
Fire is not calculable like bodies.

We keep living the same life over and over . . .
Distinction blurs like embers turning cold.
We sit beside this familiar heat
On a night so deep it could never be rehearsed.

II

Atoms

"But is it given to men to be awake on earth?"

LEV SHESTOV

The herald's voice shrieks like a Greek monster,
The pain of wire and static, the claws of fear.

We have heard the warning voice.
It was neither human nor heavenly,
Neither real nor unreal,
Neither day nor night.
It was invented.
It came from a place beyond dreams.
It is knowledge,
And we nod familiarly
As the air faints with anguish.

The children huddle in the basement and giggle.
Harry Klein has a nose that talks and wiggles.
Cathy Sampson has a sore.
War and peace and war and peace and war.

The path that goes through fire and ice
Looks neither to the left nor right.
It is the path that honors the energy
That beats in the bowels of living things.
Refreshment of heat and pain and night,
Of dew and thoughts
Inscribes the path in living hearts.

It beseeches memory and detail.
It is the actual promise.

Do not look away, inevitable pilgrim.
Do not forget to honor the energy
That is green and dies and returns
With all the decorous strength of the living.

Where a body lives, depends:
Squatters embrace ruins, garbage,
Flotsam, the artifacts of earth,
And live.

Do not speak
Do not speak of this

Fires recede, but the atom's fire
Endures beyond heat and fire.
Skies kindle desirous cities but
Rooms remain:
Cool and pure and cluttered,
Indicating the postures of tenancy.

The fire of the atom is more
Than fire, it is the eye of spirit,

The furnace of the alien gaze,
The power of pure magnitude.
It has abandoned death.

Its laugh is the sun split open,
Its tears are the sea calling
To a lost river.
Its mathematic is the force
Of impetuous logic.

Squatters stare at the newspaper ads
Before starting a fire.
Centuries of houses sit
On hills and plains and alleys.
Tomorrow brings a stick
That upholds a scrap of sheet,
Tomorrow brings forgetful
Mansions, obdurate tenancy.

An underdeputy for Nuclear Security Policy,
Mr. Keats anticipates
His boss's longueurs, loathings, and lectures
With all the startled anticipation of empathy.
An underdeputy is confidant
And tutelary, the ready idea
And thoughtful agreement,
The man's wife-man.
At lunch, the small talk of others'
Failings, cabals, the fears of the uninformed,
Enemies, glancing self-pity.

Dead fish swim on white plates.
Scented women come and go.
Social alcohol becomes oracular:
"Technology, Keats, invites protocols men
Never dreamt of, harsher sanities."
The underdeputy signals the waiter
At the last, near-confessional moment.
Camaraderie lights an earned cigarette.

Real flowers on the table—
Roses and carnations and roses

You know how much one of these
Babies costs? One of these bombers
That takes a look at Europe every night?
You work for seven lifetimes and
You couldn't buy one.
No lie.
The government's got the money
That is money.
And they got the planes, my boy,
They got the motherfucking sons of planes.
Let's get us a Coke
And I'll give you some more of the tour.

The path is a custom of the soul.
Quiet-minded, it disbelieves
The claims of disputants,
Promise-makers, theorists.
It wanders through empty lots,
Forests, fields, cracked sidewalks.
A moving way, it catches the shadows of mortality.
The custom of the path is always present.
It lives anonymously,
It dwells and departs,
Treads on worlds, sideways holy.
It cannot give proper answers to
The spirits of inquiry. It stumbles.
From moment to moment
It is moving, but it is a path,
The human custom of yearning energy.

Through the almost-tropical capital afternoon
Keats deploys terminologies, acronyms,
Assessments. Outside the building a few
Reverends hold up signs. He would like
To remind them that their welfare is
His care, that objective realities
Cannot be disputed, that the enemy
Is real and frankly cynical.

Look at the data on the terminal screen.
Sincerity, he would like to say,
Will be the death of all of us.
At 3:30 they lower their placards
And walk slowly away. A cardinal sings.
Keats prepares for his day's third meeting.

June 7

My soul is stung by probable grief
And florid indifference, as if the Lord's
Commandments were placid rhetoric.
I attest I fear to little more than
A tepid anachronism or moral superstition.
I stand in plain daylight unseen—
As if I were an angel. Forgive me, please,
My ministerial misgivings. Forgive me.
My mood is fateful; I am
No angel but an angular peacemaker,
Harrowed and anointed
By a faith I cannot communicate.
I stare in a wilting sun at that drone
Of a building, a subscription to Caesar,
And recall that power has always been this way—
Huge, stubborn, anxious to impress,
Hallowing an expedient logic,
Hoping to forget that force is
The pride of desperation.
I never admired the reputation of granite,
The eternities of capitals.
I am thankful for our Lord's rebukes,
For it is hard to tell that any
Of us are alive or that we die.

The national security is metaphysical
In the truest sense,
Demanding not only hardware
But an oratorical defense,
A permanent, rhetorical scare
To harry ontological lulls.

Possible apocalypse buttresses a more
Dreaded prospect—the enemy
Seated in our cars and planes and moods,
Dining on our impotence, free
To insult our treasured platitudes,
Evening the symbolic score.

Never and never and never—
Thus, the myth of changelessness
This vigilance so steadily repeats.
Identity is never more precious
Than when its perishing seems complete.
For empires wish to live forever,

Armored bodies immune to debt,
Despair, decay, disease—
As if only cowardice incurred death.
These postures feign and tease
Most earnestly. Our every breath
Hides an oblivious threat.

Friday afternoon in the early summer,
Herds of autos abandon the melting city.
The disaster of heat flogs
The suffering bureaucrat; Keats
And Horace (his boss) put away
The graphs, analyses, scenarios
And talk about their relaxations.
There will be gulfs of gin, balls stroked
Forcefully, adamant advantages and
Mock-plaintive cries of perfidy.
Time will recline on a veranda
And mutter pink velleities.

A breakdown in the passing lane, an accident,
An ambulance moaning defiantly:
Here is a quotient of frustration
For the most efficient psyche.
The gentlemen shift their plump buttocks,
Waylay annoyance with witticism,
Stare at their fellow refugees, discuss
The dislogic of merging highways.
An engine begins to spectacularly overheat,
The rumble of chemical steam smoking through
An ornate grill, wetting the black
Back of Interstate 405.
Two tired children begin to cry.

This rupture represents for the gentlemen
Another delaying inconvenience.
Nervous horns begin to bark.
Someone booms a filthy curse.
But magically the traffic begins to move
And the drivers know

That they are only temporary
Evacuees: the road will end peaceably.
Keats and Horace and thousands more
Will sleep in predictable beds.

Behind each numbered door
   Each desk and conference table
   Filing cabinet and attaché
Stands the grandeur of mystique.
   Power is purely formal.

Each department, enclave, section
   Harbors its prerogatives,
   Exercises the options
Of interpretive belief.

Worlds are made and rated
   Observed and downgraded
   On the surfaces of paper
At the centers of perimeters.
   Power is purely formal.

Lives are crushed and saved
   By a daily geology
   A grinding of policies
The divinity of understanding.

Intelligence eludes reason,
   Slams the drawer shut.
   Epochs of tension
Remain patently calculable
   Power is purely formal.

The imagination breeds fantasies
Horace never fails to detest.
He keeps a journal of worthless perturbations
That have come to his attention,
People roaring and ranting
Over a few misplaced emotions,
Indulging the delinquencies of metaphor.

Why not accept that whatever
Happens makes good—
If not agreeable—sense?
Why not accept this beleaguered century
For what it is—
A portentous cul-de-sac,
The scene of abandonment and remorseless invention?

Those who revel in weakness
Are as guilty as those
Who pretend we have no weakness.

This world is nasty,
Horace would like to say
One day to one of those pasty-faced
Clergymen who carry signs and write rebuking letters.
This eudaemonistic world remains unhappy.
The strategies of joy are elusive.

There is no satisfaction
In such knowledge;
Horace wishes when he looks at the sky

Or the cherry blossoms
That it were otherwise.
But it isn't, and he and
His enemies must understand
One another perfectly,
Must agree that hope
Is a human but worthless necessity.

Here is a gift
Too great to comprehend
It calls for the reverence
Due the calm miracle
The imbuing spirit
The many and the one
It is the earthgift
An absolute fruit
Turning within
The light of space
   Unbidden

Raise up the gift of thanks
Return the favor of the great
With the small
Return the unimaginable
With a voice
Discreet and plain
Return the gift with
The wealth of humility
The small voice that
Is stubborn and warm
The glad testimony
   Unbidden

Who will put the atom back?
Who will put disaster in its place,
Give Caliban a soothing speech
And Prospero his finitude?
    Oh who will do this soon?

Who will put the atom back
And let the spasm sleep?
Who will seize the fitful truth
Before the vacant dawn?
    Oh who will do this soon?

Who will put the atom back
In the customs of peace,
The orbits that move unhindered,
Unregarded, and unseen?
    Oh who will do this soon?

Ask a woman, man, nation,
God, and listen for an answer.
Listen for the sounds of minds
As they consider what is pure;
The ancient, flowing step; the atom.

Throw weight, overkill, cruise missile,
Strategic deterrence, ground-launched
Multiple independently targetable
Reentry vehicles, Jupiter,
Tomahawk, Pershing, and Thor:
The terms and names trickle like sand
Into the gullet of understanding.
A grafting genius works here,
Part accuracy, part bluff, part
Anonymity, part command.
Words are slaves, supinely elastic,
Mumbling most obsequiously,
Usable and disposable.
Words are the walls between
The unallowable and the actual,
Between the mind and the voice.
Words are placid signs,
Their accuracy may be enjoined
Against them quite subtly.
Words are their own enemies.
Keats sits at his desk and ponders
Tactics, the technical stance that
Signifies adamant willingness.
Keats combs his folders and charts.
Sometimes he thinks he is an alchemist.
"The close edge of nuclear
Proximity reduces combative hegemony.
The instant aura of quick exchange
Predicates protracted
Mutually assertive power displays."
The difficulty inveigles Keats.
He looks past the easy subterfuge
To a more sonorous truth,

The Latinate timbre that announces
A finer turn in the annals
Of the speechless muse.

Airman Hawkins opens a Budweiser
And stares at the constellation of planes
Each one of which has a woman's name.
The night above the guardian airman is
A harvest of stars, the dwindling of light.
He thinks of his girlfriend Lula Mae,
Of the hair on certain parts of her body,
Of how when she's beneath him she will
Call out his name. He throws an empty
At the plodding night and opens another,
Tries to remember he is waiting for a war.

Before he passes out he wonders who
It was who thought this shit up and what for?

In the brig with the sickos, thieves, druggies,
Airman Hawkins senses that this is no comedy,
That the trouble he didn't want has come for sure.
A black man, as his father would have said,
Is born with trouble without looking for more.
Now he has committed a punishable crime—
Partying with sixteen bombers on a Tuesday night.

And weren't the planes still there?
Who's gonna rob 'em?
Will they send that black lieutenant in
To talk with him?

The minister throws a few reminders to
His flock, threads inattention with the needle of wit,
Smiles and decorously thunders and smiles
And fidgets before that absence
Of stringency, his God.

Once in cathedrals, God's light illumined
All manner of faces, God's light explained
The disease of men and women. Pilgrim steps
Were drowned in seas of air and light and bells.
The steps of time were lost,
The songs of choirs rose and vanished.
The soul, the vessel of darkest light,
Was tossed upon the waves of colored light
And found its beacon in its foundering,
In its night.

The minister enters his sanctuary
    on a weekday,
Looks at the stillness about him,
And feels the hand of the blank,
    consoling light.
The firmament of blinding impulse,
The blanket of sin that comforts all blindness,
The body's arrogance of time's comfort,
The arrogance of assured words:
Puritan hands have struck that light
    to little avail.
It is the light that has shone on every morning
After Eden, myth and no-myth,
Workmanlike, recently scientific.
How easy (the minister reflects)
The light makes it to forget.

Placards, vigils, marches, a couple
Of cops in sunglasses calculating
Their overtime, maybe enough money
For a new outboard.
　　The performance
Of outrage is soothingly ritual.
The clerics and students do not flinch.
They are scrupulously glad
Although their songs and silences speak
To notions long ago outvoted.
　　Deliberately
They go where they should not go.

The cops wish all the weirdos
Were this discreet.

The grin of matter as it spins through time,
The ecstatic couplings and collisions,
The multitudinous deaths: all inform
The voice of accurate awe.

Nothing is too much, the abundance of sex
Is mathematic, casual, impolitic.

Everything alive and humming,
Whether heard or not, all things
Making a flat dizzying music,
Sparks of time distended, arcing slowly.

Impossible to notice
And still get on with life, impossible.
Not to listen is to feign life,
Not to listen is to hobble praise.
Nursery rhyme alive
The song skips through time,
Fierce and rapt, exigent as sunshine.

June 14

Scorn cackles
Like an anxious crow. Scorn says, "Fool."
I have frequented jails before and met
The remarks of criminals, their sad
Bewildered rage, their broken humor,
As if in their contempt they were freed.
"The reverend here's a trespasser on
Government property, wants to arrest Uncle
Sam and got himself arrested instead."
Is man as hapless a creature as he seems?
Must I seek the old Jehovah,
The grandeur of willful abasement?
And why do I fear our Lord's displeasure?
Why do I place myself at the center
Of His universe? I am an outside orbit,
A fleck of matter pinioned by spirit—
But I hate these reductionisms
And so, I must recall, does our Lord.
It is the more of me and these men
Around me that is troubling, the gift
Of grace which rusts with indifference.
It is the more of me that is beguiling,
All the doors of possibility that beckon
With the summer of God's creation.
Reverence dwells in us but it lives so
Bitterly, so fearfully, ever protesting its
Knowledge, its station, its designs.
Necessity is the failure of love.

Airman Hawkins' Dream—
Exhibition A

In the beginning was a bird with a bomb
In its beak. The sky was gunmetal,
The earth was wet ashes. The bird was deathblack
But bigger than any bird you saw and powerful strong.
It never stopped waving its wings.

You never get near to a bird
Because a bird is the last wildest thing.
It doesn't want friendly men.
You get near it, you feel
It bad, the panic.
Oh the bird needs the whole
Damn sky, each inch of it!
I watch the bird and I can't fly.
My feet are lead; I am a statueman,
No-name but frozen the same.
I see the bird's eyes and they are hollow.
I am a statue but I know that bird is blind.

The bomb is bigger than the bird
So the bird could never bear it
Yet it seems to do it. I knew the bird
Was bound to fall because it was only
A bird, it was only so strong.
There was only so much wind.

Even the sky began to seem small.
Would the statue of me begin to move?
Away and away the bird flew.

Under flourescent suns
The reticent authors
Of impartial global death
Embroider calculations
While discussing backgammon,
Cuisines, the ups and downs
Of their perishable health.

Exonerations are unnecessary.
As maxims say,
The truth is its own reward.
The atom more and less exists:
Coherent confusion, mobile
Package, like God
The ravisher of metaphor.

Science is the vindication
Of material temptation,
The drone of miracles.
Devoted men evaluate
Trajectories, payloads,
Strangely frail symmetries.

Their children love them
Though a few when they
Are grown up no longer
Understand their fathers
Revile them experience agonies.

The fathers shake
Their heads. Who can
Avoid investigating the real?
What good does it do to pretend?

Numbers buzz in the mind
Of matter. No secrets.
The distances of intimacies
Are measured by instruments.
Occasionally sons and daughters weep
And shriek. Large thoughts are
Hard to hold. A modest lust
Licks the corridors of time,
Ascends into the plodding heaven of equations.

Rome, that radiant sewer of officious vigor,
Thugs and rhetoricians, posturing senators,
Officeseekers and slaves,
Beckons to Horace in all its prolix eternity.
It is a whore's cash smile—
Yet dying that long bewildering death
Seems heaven beside this managing of suddenness,
A lifetime eying the supramundane flash.

What would one of those original, ancient
Bureaucrats have said to this peculiar department?
To perpetuate offices, revise
Inefficient procedures, praise via
Memoranda the sanity of inertia:
Such would be the trodden ground.
But more than that,
To meet civilization's constant *crise*
De nerfs, the babble of petitioners,
Sycophants, what each age calls "thinkers,"
To meet these threats evenhandedly,
Punctiliously, as if nothing were new
Under this summer sun—that is the point
Of honor that waters weary hearts.
Anonymity is by definition dismissive.
No one honors those souls who ask
The abyss its name and rank.
Presumption and snide humility—that is
The common charge leveled at Roman,
American, no doubt at Russian too.
Injustice is the badge of duty.

Horace hears the sighs of his predecessors,
The mass of derelictions and corrections.

Rome cracked like a vase, shattered to
The touch, but this empire of money
And good intentions must be otherwise.
There is no choice. Horace
Holds up a world not of his device
And cannot flinch and will not.

Public murder becomes popular
With the masses and cognoscenti alike.
Assassins and gladiators compete
For brief attention. Even jesters are done in:
John Lennon the rock'n'roller,
Nero's literary crowd invited
To swill poison—
Death no longer death but an event.
The publicist's apotheosis of personality turns
Gods into factory goods, bestows
The lineaments of eternity upon moments.
If the posters wept, if the emperor's
Favorites had only realized their danger,
If the millions of applauding fans
Held their eager hands . . .
Fear is no proper life,
Say the Romans staring
At the seasoned cup. Fear is no life,
Says the happily howling guitarist.
Manias split time:
Atoms are ripe fruit.
Fear replies in the quietest eyes,
In torpid emperors,
Artistes, all the anguished gunmen.

The rebel rocker Lennon
Makes his music among
Stacks of machines, nails
His voice to a spinning dream,
Welcomes more unwieldy years.

When wishes become heroes
Anthems occur accordingly.
Longings stutter then flash
Into the thin strong
Flesh of song.

Lennon cheers for peace,
Acknowledges his soul
Occasionally stinks like all souls.
The man is too well-known.
Multitudes are fans of peace;

Even underdeputies hear tunes
On radios or catch a bit
Of what is coming from
Their teenagers' rooms:
Bright melody of hope.

Lennon screams for joy and fear.
Look how real time is
How a singer lives and dies
How a song ends one moment
In a fit of contrivance.

There is a party on this planet.
Day and night there is dancing
Inside rooms and heads.

There is pleasure on this planet
Only music describes.

The brisk beat of modern natives
Harangues undone hearts.
Lennon proclaims opportunities:
A tapping foot that wants
So badly to live.

A remote ordeal rumors every mind:
It is the land where warheads stare like dead eyes,
Where thousands of dead eyes stare
Into the day that is night when men and women
Are children and children are men and women.
It is where a tiny fist pounds on a door
And is not heard.
The ordeal never reaches the day.

It is a fairy tale
Where curiosity has played a trick on men and women.
Could it be?

The streets are full of supplicants,
Marchers for peace, singers of Lennon's songs,
But knowledge cannot abate.
Remove the curse, the people chant,
As if knowledge were impiety.

All the people are one person with
A common sinning father.
The facts present a remote death
To which the mind condescends.

A tiny fist pounds on a door.
It is brave as a voice. It is cowardly.
It hears rumors that are hidden.
Remove the curse, remove the curse.

Airman Hawkins has spoken with an angel.
She is terse, lyrical, pensive.
She is brown and smells like new hay.
She is sisterly.
There are too many loyalties and not enough bonds.
There are nations, platoons, families, marriages,
   leagues, squadrons, beliefs.
There is one active earth. It is quiet.
It is damp in the night grass around
   the landing strips.
Airman Hawkins sips at his Budweiser
And tells the angel about his home.
There is a broken step there, a catalpa tree,
Pictures of Jesus—he was black sometimes
And he was white.
The angel understands.
Why is he here beside these planes?
What is his uniform?
His heart is a well no bucket has touched.
The angel says she will read his heart.
It is dusty earth that heart.
Listen for steps in the air, paths,
Do not laugh at angels, their digressions.

In the middle of the night
There is neither left nor right
In the castle's highest tower
There is neither day nor hour

Approaching voices can be heard
Clever tactics conceal the roads
Each remains free to say
Life has always been this way

When was logic ever news?
When were visions ever true?
When the stars cried out for grief
When nothing happened beyond belief

June 15

I greet anguish, a tocsin ringing in
My soul, my vitals caught and wrung.
Devil, devil, devil, how is it we cannot
Name you, how is it we slight you?
This planet is God's gesture, the logos
Of ardor. These wilting days
I spy the springs of shame.
Ministers, I think, are specially culpable
With their upright hypocrisies, Biblical slogans,
Their boundless willingness. Jail teaches this—
Our assurances make no difference.
Doubt must be my soil, the fearfulness
That calls on God and waits.
I will not subscribe to our peculiar liberated
Cruelty—that glib approbation
Of all humanity's inclinations, the gift of bombs.
God is the gift we must see if we
Are to earn it.
God crouches in the night and waits
As we must wait.
Our joy is no more than indifference,
The body's quick subservience.
Our days are dyed with an honest darkness:
That is my hope.

The emperors dicker, chew on their talky mortality.
More than men and less than men,
No woman violates them.
Once there were dragons, ogres, demons.
Negotiators explain their proposals,
The interballistic test,
Riddles of legalisms.
As in fairy tales
Death results from a lack of imagination.
The emperors refuse ransom.
Intently they ask purported questions,
Blow down precipices,
Assume there are no surprises.

A parable would knock them over.
One parable wielded by a woman at dusk would ruin them,
One parable that is at the gates of everyone's lips.
It is the story of the woman who stood calmly,
The heroine who refused idolatry.
Life is the invisible thing, the heroine says,
The shadow of monoliths and houseflies.
Its pulse cannot be suppressed.
Men do not impress this tingling breath.
She dances with her broom, sends back the prince's ring.
The emperors engage stolid exigencies,
Negotiate terminably.
Everywhere on this planet a parable is waiting.

Augustus never would have allowed this
(Writes Horace). I mean not only
The atrabilious cant, the attitudinizing—
Which, after all, always define the political—
But this spewing of invisible blood,
The impossible protestations. We will die—
Must we hear this as news and insight?
Augustus never paraded mortalities
For the rabble's applause, choosing rather to
Query those quaint, retired gods as
Custom demanded. The gods were experts
But quiet, cunningly perverse.
We lack such advice and claw at peace
As though it were the flesh of life.
Nothing saves men and women,
Nothing heals them,
Nothing soothes the anxious abyss
But lies and more lies. Augustus
Knew that peace is oppression,
A foot on your opponent's throat,
A sword held aloft, waiting
To do its work. Augustus, who charmed
And discarded geniuses, smiled from the depths
Of a shrewdness too frank to confess.

June 16

Sin, that stalking word, relic
Of less perfect centuries, upbraids me.
There I may find the logic
That escapes me, the apt aspersion.
There I may find our tempering.
Men and women pace the orderly streets,
Scene of a matter-of-fact abyss,
A blithe nothingness.
I must cry out, I must find my voice
In this absent darkness.
A few distressed seminarians and ministers protest:
The body without a soul
Is but a plaything, the toy of mechanisms
And theories, preening technologies.
The body without a soul
Is but the passion of history.
God's lightning sits in the atom and waits.
Bodies crack and break like
The husks of ancient insects.
This pride that works from day
To day has sucked the marrow of infinity.

I speak a tale that sunlight heals,
I am told by my better-adjusted visitors.

I am caught by questions,
Hanged perpetually. Old-fashioned thunder.

Keats tunes his words carefully,
Searching for the middle ground,
The place where nightmare
And common sense neatly meet.

What should not be said, must be said.
What should not be borne, must be borne.
There must be a talent for necessity
In certain officials, a fatalist genius.

Keats searches for concepts, as if glass
Never broke nor fire burnt.
There are higher arguments than matter,
There are higher threats than death.

He knows, of course, the truth.
A child knows that truth.
But truth is never singular:
Each word is calmly multiple,

There is no pure, mimetic mirror.
Keats tunes his words carefully;
He lulls blinding eternities,
Practices disutopian notes.

All this must be, he says.
Near-salvation lies in near-formality,
The word that swallows dread
Like a well-cooked heart,

The word that is already lost.
Keats finesses and probes.
Horace goes home early on
Another muggy mid-afternoon.

Roman violence counterfeited
Blood without motives
The stagey screams of machines
   movies

Each spectator an emperor
The gladiators hewing flesh
The lion's paw shredding flesh
   like paper

The designs the dabbles of blood
   trace in the sand
The lust and commentaries

One emperor after another
Adducing missiles
Investing sullen innocence

Blood without conflicts
Civilization demanding nourishments
Victims who salute the emperor

Monsters have human flaws
The gladiator hops on one foot
   caught in his own net
The tiger leaps
   enraged

The distance between the seat
   and the sand
Between the seat and the screen
Between the life and the death

The distance spun like a web
Entrapping violence
Frozen millions

The lion's paw

At the bottom of the bottle of beer,
At the bottom of the glass of gin,
A staring face is found again.

The fearful distractions wilt.
The twinges and twitches go home.
Each gulp has its loosening logic.
The feelings that have sat and waited
Speak with strange articulation:

What can a body ever know?
What can a body do?
Where in this barred world can a soul fly off to?

"Lennon considers renunciation,"
Never made the headlines.
Nonetheless, the famous performer
Wished to divest his anxious self,
Wished to relieve his knowledge,
Appurtenances, obligations,
And face the world with the silly
Candor of nakedness.
First came the shouts of drumming joy,
Sensations of girls and boys;
Then came the perishing world;
Then the private envoy—imagination.
Emperor-like he absolved his public.
"Anger never brought a man peace."

At the bottom of skeptical being
Rests a belief in the visible invisible,
A brick of substance, Roman solidity.

The world is not a dream, the atom swears.
Men and women cannot see or hear or know.
They are blind and deaf and ignorant.

They gambol in the fields of life. They guess.
Some practical enchantment is at work.
Some subdued force is ever-busy.

What kingdom is it you cannot enter,
Where there are no doors or windows or gates?
It is a taunting place, the atom,

A hell and heaven place, above,
Inside, and below the real,
But unreal, an infinite model.

It is a place that destroys all places.
It is the final, moveable kingdom.
Men and women cannot see or hear or know

What causes the tangible worlds. They guess.
They dissect their voracious vertigo.
For men and women are ever-falling,

Maplessly certain, solid bodies,
Whose knowledge remains credulity,
The breath of life casually esteemed.

The Romans had their Greeks,
Americans their business,
Russians their ideology.
Was there ever, Horace wonders,
An actual civilization,
Or is that notion nothing more
Than the tonic of social-climbing nations?
Ideals are ludicrous
But comfortably impotent and preferable
To the lithe mumblings of senators
Who want the nation's defense to be
And not to be. Profess loathing and charity,
Horace would say, it's the same to me,
The lackey who greases your self-deceptions.
Keats manipulates words, creates small kingdoms,
But the price he pays is belief in words,
Belief in his own conceptions; whereas
Horace is calmly pagan, awaiting nothing,
Applauding no one, alone with all
The ardent brevities, formally convivial.
Whoever said this world was meant "forever,"
Whoever grasped that cheap, romantic word?
Let death counter death frankly,
Let there be a skull inside every hope:
Not that Poe-like death's head but
The matter-of-factness of bones,
The overlooked rigidity that makes
All this fluency possible.
Nations want to elude their deaths,
Pretend there are no deaths.
Idealisms invoke cataclysms.
But death is small and daily, approachable
And patient, like a man at a desk
Who offers calm and undeceived answers.

In the brig there is all the time in the world.
Airman Hawkins reads his father's letter
For the thousandth time, his father the preacher
And he the only son, the son of sons.
A preacher man is something more than a man
And less than a man, a fiery man
But a heaven man, a strong man
But a soft man, a man of God's only words.
God never spoke to this airman;
He never but whistled. He just let this
Airman be, let him stand there at night
Watching the planes and sky.
Doesn't a mind get to wondering then,
Doesn't a body feel alone out there,
Doesn't a heart start thinking?
A preacher man is no drinking man
But his son is something else, his son
Wants to let go sometimes of this world
And the others. His son wants to let go
And forget how a man must be a man.

There could be killing like the Bible's killing:
Tribes slaughtered, plagues,
Rivers dry as chalk. Those planes
Could be in a preacher man's Bible,
Those bombs and missiles and guns. There is
A man who sits and waits, whose mind is a trigger,
Who is all men. That man is in
The preacher's Bible. Cain and Absalom.

The airman knows something his father doesn't.
He has met that man.

June 19 (after three days of prayer)

The long death of reverence, ashen tongues . . .
My opposition lies in other directions;
Without the tie of praise there is neither strength
    nor grace.
I seek the alleluia
That sleeps in the souls of men and women,
That sings of our Lord who moves all things,
Who is neither scrutable nor sized.
I see a world each day
That witty man could never have made.
I see fractions, the powers of chance,
But what chance
Of such fullness returning?
God does not deal in duplicates—
That is His glory.
I praise this dust, the weary day-end
Steps of men and women, all things that are
Not things but paths of spirit, God's breath.

The inappropriateness of human actions
As on the morning of a battle
A day of financial panic
A night of anxious liaisons
Oh weariness and freshness
So strangely mixed
    unseasonable blooms
Why does the world remain
Amid the inappropriateness of human questions?
It is difficult to accept gifts
To practice a heartfelt etiquette
It is easier to throw an imperial fit
Which is your favorite planet?
What wind do you prefer?
What sort of sunrise?
Emperors make improvements
Dedicate arches and oversee urinals
The dawn breeze stirs soft sheets
Someone gladly moans
A little sound of release and forgetting
That is not heard

Held like an insect in the botanizer's
Pincers, the emperor Marcus Aurelius
Does not wriggle rebelliously but praises
Resignation, the sanguine wisdom of what is.
In the northern marshes fever awaits him.
He neither tarries nor hurries;
Death is a deliberate obligation.

Admirers and critics say the same thing,
Virtue consumes Marcus. He is waxen,
Earthen, iron. He is long-faced and bridled,
Abhors the froth of poetry.

The poet Horace found the Stoics amusing,
Their habit of saluting
The genius of what cannot be avoided,
Their lack of cavalier
Relish for the chances of sweethearts and wine.
Dull but honest, thorough if narrow,
They might watch the empire expire and merely sigh.

Poems were mostly deceits and flatteries,
The ravings of clever weaklings. Marcus's children
All dying except for the brute Commodus.
Bad joke upon bad joke—that was the learned
Design of destiny. Disease was wise.
The emperor wept dispassionately.

Obedience is the curse of boredom,
God is alive and selling real estate in Brooklyn—
The sort of graffiti that attracted Lennon
While walking through the imperial squalor
Of New York City. The streets rich with actual
Touts, panders, hoodlums, the possessed
And dispossessed, carnal and carnival, everywhere
The uptight-white-man-dead-hand-fearful.
All there for the viewing and the taking—
Shot of amphetamine, hiss of heroin,
Languor of marijuana, the world of
Sensate oblivion empires accentuate.
Quiver and drone, vibrate and thrum,
So many so casually undone.
Crying and laughing when
Hyperbole becomes standard contempt:
Jokes protest plagues, money, mayors,
Varieties of sex, technological accidents.
The impotent stand up each day and salute
Their resolute dignity, the wanton strength that
Makes them incontestably human.
People whistle in the street, hum the songs
Of John Lennon, march and sway and glide.
Helter-skelter alive, helter-skelter alive.

Dear Father Hawkins,
    I have stopped taking orders.
I know that this is going to pain you.
To you it will seem the devil, disrespect
And near to murder, one more gone-crazy black man.
You may not try to understand but
I have sat in this cell for weeks with
Nothing to do but think. Repent, you'd say,
Repent your foolishness, childish pride,
National negligence while there is time.
But I'm finished here and will stay finished.
I never want to step back in that line.
The stars were speaking to me that night,
Talking about being alive, about
Bombers, airmen, the home of the sky.
I was drunken but now am sober,
And I don't want to study orders anymore.
I know that I don't have to listen
The way I've had to listen, I don't have to follow.
Sometimes a soldier has got to become a man
And it's not always like he planned
Back when he was a boy. Beginning is hard.
I have disgraced myself and you. I have sinned—
But not the way the lawyer says.
Do you know how little we are? That is what
The stars told me, Father.
      Your son (sober)

The newspapers full of speeches and protests,
   demonologies.
Horace makes a face at his too-weak coffee—
The tepidness of bartered solutions,
The aversion to difficulty.

"Dear editor, If only you would listen to me.
I am good and peaceful and honorable.
I am serious."
Oh innocent *hypocrite écrivain,*
Who are you? Come forward, you who rue
This stalwart agenda for destruction.
You are my brother or sister. You drive a car,
You go to work, you travel on planes,
Have obligations, theorize, worry.
Who will turn his face away?
Who will look thoroughly?
Who will provide the absolving assurances?
Horace makes himself read more words:
They are laudable sentiments.
He rises from the table deliberately.

Ideas put a bright face on torment.
Horace wonders where to take his next vacation.

June 21

For penance—the rooting
Out of preaching eloquence. It is only the dearest words,
The burrs of truth, that will do:

The small steps a stranger takes uncertainly,
Plain tenderness,
The recusant key of conscience.

Admit the unanswerable.
I know this silting blood knows nothing—
It is a right sum for a man professing religion.

Small steps, the accuracy of obedience
To what I never will comprehend.
My pleasure is the light within darkness.

It is unannounced; it asks nothing.
I see and am unafraid. What can
I say of God's love for our suffering?

It is valiant, outleaping the unseen atom,
Outshining all visible brilliance.
Amid so much brittle glory

Something humbling adheres:
There are tasks of atonement,
This river of energy, days that end.

About the Author

Baron Wormser is the author of two previous volumes of poetry, *The White Words* (Houghton Mifflin, 1983) and *Good Trembling* (1985). He lives in Norridgewock, Maine, where he works as a librarian.